This journal belongs to

_____

_____

Email us your reviews and questions at
theanytimejournal@gmail.com

© The Anytime Journal. All rights reserved. No part of this publication may be reproduced, distributed, or transmitted in any form or by any means, including photocopying, recording, or other electronic or mechanical methods, without prior written permission of the publisher.

Hi there!

I am so excited for you to use this journal as a guide to appreciate the beauty within your life.

Gratitude

We have heard, time after time, how we should be more grateful for the things/people/experiences we have in life. After all, our goal in life is to be happy. Everyone wants to be happy - happy with their job, their relationships, their finances, and themselves. How else would we know how good we have it in life if we didn't stop for a moment to really appreciate the beauty within our lives.

"Gratitude turns what we have into enough, and more. It turns denial into acceptance, chaos into order, confusion into clarity...it makes sense of our past, brings peace for today, and creates a vision for tomorrow."
— *Melody Beattie*

Affirmations

Affirmations are exercises for our minds. It's like going to the gym and working on your abs. If you work out long enough you start to see those defined muscles peeping through.

Affirmations train your mind to believe whatever it is that you want it to believe by repeating "I am this" or "I am that". Your mind cannot differentiate between reality and imagination. It will believe whatever you tell it. The more you repeat your affirmations, the more dominant those thoughts become.

Using the combinations of the emotion of gratitude and the action of affirmations, you will recognize yourself as the powerful being you truly are.

"Every time you speak, you are either building up yourself for the better or you are limiting yourself for the worse. Words carry power, therefore before you speak out, speak in... and test your words!"
— *Israelmore Ayivor*

Why 21 days?

How often have you heard that if you do something for 21 days consecutively, it becomes a habit?

21 days is the perfect amount of time. It's neither too short nor too long. I believe that 21 days is just enough for anyone to stay on track once they pick a goal they want to achieve. That is why this journal is split into four 21-day challenges. Each time you complete a challenge, it's a smart victory worth celebrating. You will feel like you know yourself a little bit better than you first started. Then you repeat for another 21 days, then another.....

However, some days you don't get a chance to write and that is OK. Everyone has one of those days so don't be hard on yourself if you do miss a day. This journal is meant for you to have some "Me Time" and connect with yourself.

I hope that journaling becomes a habit that you can keep up with every day, but completing a 21-day challenge or a set of 21 entries every time is sure to keep you motivated.

How to use this journal?

There are a few more unique approaches to the way this journal is set up. A combination of gratitude, affirmations, and self-discovery questions being obvious reasons, but as you may have noticed, the setup is very different.

For each day, it is asked that after you write down what you are grateful for, you are to write an affirmation that will go with that gratification.

Because I am so grateful for this, therefore, I am that.
The reason behind this is that whenever you think, see, hear, or use that "thing" you are grateful for, you will be able to remember the affirmation you wrote and hopefully repeat it to yourself.

Use the following examples to help you:

1. I am so grateful for kids **because** they bring so much joy into my life.
I am a good mom. **or** I am important to my family.

2. I am so grateful for having a job **because** it provides me with financial stability.
I am abundant. **or** I am a magnet for success.

3. I am so grateful for my bed **because** it keeps me warm and cozy at night.
I am comfortable. **or** I am deserving of all good things in life.

I've included a list of some affirmations you can use to help you get started.

Remember, write what resonates with you.

How to use this journal?

Followed by the gratitude/affirmations are some questions. The questions vary each day to keep things interesting. Some days you will find a task that is to be completed for that day while other days it's questioned in regards to your day to help you be more present, while other days it might be some short questions about you.

Remember, these questions can be answered regardless of the time you write in this journal.

The 'ABOUT MY DAY' part of the journal can be used in a few different ways depending on when you are writing in the journal. For example, if you are writing in the morning, you can use this space to write out your to-do list of the day. If you are writing later on in the day or before bed, you can use this space to highlight the events of the day. If you are feeling creative, use this space to draw. It's about you and your day. Express your emotions about your day in any way you feel comfortable.

The "I LOVE' part of the journal is to express a bit more gratitude using a different set of terms. You can write a few words to write what it is that you love but just hold on to the emotion of gratitude and love that you feel as you are writing.
Some examples of what you can write:

I LOVE:
- a warm cup of coffee
- long hot shower
- naps
- listening to music.

Affirmations for Self-Love

I am calm, kind, and positive.
I am happy.
I am abundant.
I am comfortable.
I am strong and brave.
I am powerful.
I am important.
I am enough.
I am unique and have so much to offer this world
I am in charge of my life.
I always have everything I need to be happy.
I am perfect, whole, and complete.
I am always in the right place at the right time.
I am present in every moment.
I am rich in health, wealth, and love.
I always have everything I need.
I am in control of my happiness.
I am an amazing person.
I am happy with what I have.
I am proud of myself.
I am confident and determined.
I believe in myself.
I accept myself for who I am.
Today, and every day, I choose to be happy.
I deserve to be loved.
I love myself more every day.
I learn and grow from every experience
I can do anything I put my mind to.
I forgive myself for my mistakes.
I have everything I need at this time.
I see the beauty in everything and everyone.
I have the power to make my dreams come true.

Affirmations for Career/Job/Money/Success

I am happy and successful.
I am a leader.
I am wealthy and abundant.
I am confident and determined.
I am excited and enthusiastic about my job/career.
I am an achiever.
I am in charge of my life.
I am a money magnet.
I am a manget for success.
I am worthy of all the richness I desire.
I am so excited because all of my dreams are coming true.
I am a good person who deserves success and happiness.
I am very motivated, driven, and ambitious.
I am surrounded by abundance.
I am resilient, persistent, and dedicated.
I am destined for greatness.
I am passionate about constantly being better and more successful.
I inspire others to be their best self.
I give myself permission to be wealthy.
I have the power to create success and build the wealth I desire.
I achieve everything and anything I put my mind to.
I believe in myself.
I love what I do.
I am constantly presented with new opportunities for success.
I see happiness and success wherever I go.
Success comes effortlessly to me.
Everywhere I go I create joy, love, and success.
I have faith in myself and in my abilities
I am enjoying everything I have, and this constitutes my abundance.

Affirmations for Health

I am healthy.
I am healthy, happy, and radiant.
I am strong.
I am getting stronger each day.
I am constantly discovering new ways to improve my health.
I take care of my body.
I listen to my body.
I love and appreciate my body.
My body is healed, restored, and filled with energy.
My happy thoughts help create my healthy body.

Affirmations for Relationships

I am an amazing _____ (mom, dad, wife, husband, son, daughter)
I am working hard to support my family.
I am a positive role model for my children.
I am deserving of love and patience.
I am worthy of the love I receive from my family.
I am doing my best and that is enough.
I am loved.
I am blessed with an incredible family.
I am enough.
I am happy and grateful for having loving people in my life
I respect my _____ and I respect myself.
Love is all around me, it's everywhere I go.
I love being with people who bring out the best in me.
I love that my relationships are in harmony with my highest good.
My family loves and appreciates me.
All my relationships are now loving and harmonious.

Make a list of your own affirmations to use:

Make a list of your own affirmations to use:

21-DAY *journaling challenge #1*

DATE:_____

Before you begin, close your eyes and take three deep breaths to relax yourself.

WRITE 3 THINGS YOU ARE GRATEFUL FOR TODAY AND WHY. THEN WRITE AN AFFIRMATION TO GO WITH EACH GRATITUDE.

1. I am so grateful for _____

_____

I am _____

_____

2. I am so grateful for _____

_____

I am _____

_____

3. I am so grateful for _____

_____

I am _____

_____

READ EACH ONE 3 TIMES!

TODAY I AM PROUD OF MYSELF FOR:

ABOUT MY DAY:

MY GOAL FOR THIS WEEK IS:

"One life. One chance."
— The shiniest star in the sky

How would you describe yourself to someone? Include physical details, your personality, the different roles you play in your daily life.

DATE:_____

Before you begin, close your eyes and take three deep breaths to relax yourself.

WRITE 3 THINGS YOU ARE GRATEFUL FOR TODAY AND WHY. THEN WRITE AN AFFIRMATION TO GO WITH EACH GRATITUDE.

1. I am so grateful for _____
_____

I am _____
_____

2. I am so grateful for _____
_____

I am _____
_____

3. I am so grateful for _____
_____

I am _____
_____

READ EACH ONE 3 TIMES!

ONE THING THAT I WANT TO CHANGE OR IMPROVE ABOUT MYSELF BY THE END OF THE 21-DAY CHALLENGE:

ABOUT MY DAY:

TASK OF THE DAY:

Put your phone away 1 hour before you go to bed.

"The hard days are what make you stronger."
— Aly Raisman

Write out your bucket list.
Do you want to accomplish these by a certain age?

DATE:_____

Before you begin, close your eyes and take three deep breaths to relax yourself.

WRITE 3 THINGS YOU ARE GRATEFUL FOR TODAY AND WHY. THEN WRITE AN AFFIRMATION TO GO WITH EACH GRATITUDE.

1. I am so grateful for _____
_____

I am _____
_____

2. I am so grateful for _____
_____

I am _____
_____

3. I am so grateful for _____
_____

I am _____
_____

READ EACH ONE 3 TIMES!

**FINISH THIS SENTENCE:
I LOVE...**

ABOUT MY DAY:

MY FAVOURITE MOVIE IS:

"Talk to yourself like you would to someone you love."
- Brené Brown

Write a letter to someone who inspires you. If possible, would you send this letter to them?

DATE:_____

Before you begin, close your eyes and take three deep breaths to relax yourself.

WRITE 3 THINGS YOU ARE GRATEFUL FOR TODAY AND WHY. THEN WRITE AN AFFIRMATION TO GO WITH EACH GRATITUDE.

1. I am so grateful for _____
_____

I am _____
_____

2. I am so grateful for _____
_____

I am _____
_____

3. I am so grateful for _____
_____

I am _____
_____

READ EACH ONE 3 TIMES!

HOW DO I FEEL RIGHT NOW?

ABOUT MY DAY:

MY FAVOURITE SONG IS:

"Everything you can imagine is real."
— Pablo Picasso

Which house chores would you rather do: cook, wash dishes, clean out the garage, mow the lawn, clean the bathroom, or vacuum the house?

DATE:_____

Before you begin, close your eyes and take three deep breaths to relax yourself.

WRITE 3 THINGS YOU ARE GRATEFUL FOR TODAY AND WHY. THEN WRITE AN AFFIRMATION TO GO WITH EACH GRATITUDE.

1. I am so grateful for _____
_____

I am _____
_____

2. I am so grateful for _____
_____

I am _____
_____

3. I am so grateful for _____
_____

I am _____
_____

READ EACH ONE 3 TIMES!

TODAY I WANT TO...

ABOUT MY DAY:

ONE COMPLIMENT I WANT TO GIVE MYSELF TODAY:

"The purpose of our lives is to be happy."
— *Dalai Lama*

What emotion do you try to avoid? Anger, sadness, jealousy, etc
What triggers this emotion? How do you overcome it?

DATE:_____

Before you begin, close your eyes and take three deep breaths to relax yourself.

WRITE 3 THINGS YOU ARE GRATEFUL FOR TODAY AND WHY. THEN WRITE AN AFFIRMATION TO GO WITH EACH GRATITUDE.

1. I am so grateful for _____
_____

I am _____
_____

2. I am so grateful for _____
_____

I am _____
_____

3. I am so grateful for _____
_____

I am _____
_____

READ EACH ONE 3 TIMES!

MY STRONGEST QUALITY:

ABOUT MY DAY:

MY WEAKEST QUALITY:

"Life is not a problem to be solved, but a reality to be experienced."
— Soren Kierkegaard

Write about why you started this journal.

DATE:_____

Before you begin, close your eyes and take three deep breaths to relax yourself.

WRITE 3 THINGS YOU ARE GRATEFUL FOR TODAY AND WHY. THEN WRITE AN AFFIRMATION TO GO WITH EACH GRATITUDE.

1. I am so grateful for _____
_____

I am _____
_____

2. I am so grateful for _____
_____

I am _____
_____

3. I am so grateful for _____
_____

I am _____
_____

READ EACH ONE 3 TIMES!

DID I ACHIEVE MY GOAL FOR THE WEEK?

ABOUT MY DAY:

ONE AMAZING THING THAT HAPPENED IN THE LAST 7 DAYS?

"Our only limitations are those we set up in our own minds."
— *Napoleon Hill*

What did someone tell you about yourself that you didn't know or notice before? Is it something you do or a certain way you act?

DATE:_____

Before you begin, close your eyes and take three deep breaths to relax yourself.

WRITE 3 THINGS YOU ARE GRATEFUL FOR TODAY AND WHY. THEN WRITE AN AFFIRMATION TO GO WITH EACH GRATITUDE.

1. I am so grateful for _____

_____

I am _____

_____

2. I am so grateful for _____

_____

I am _____

_____

3. I am so grateful for _____

_____

I am _____

_____

READ EACH ONE 3 TIMES!

TODAY I AM PROUD OF MYSELF FOR:	ABOUT MY DAY:
MY GOAL FOR THIS WEEK IS:	

"Everything you can imagine is real."
— *Pablo Picasso*

The most terrifying/challenging moment of my life was . . .
How did that moment impact the rest of your life?

DATE:_____

Before you begin, close your eyes and take three deep breaths to relax yourself.

WRITE 3 THINGS YOU ARE GRATEFUL FOR TODAY AND WHY. THEN WRITE AN AFFIRMATION TO GO WITH EACH GRATITUDE.

1. I am so grateful for _____

_____

I am _____

_____

2. I am so grateful for _____

_____

I am _____

_____

3. I am so grateful for _____

_____

I am _____

_____

READ EACH ONE 3 TIMES!

TODAY I FORGIVE OR LET GO OF:

ABOUT MY DAY:

TASK OF THE DAY:

Meditate for 10 minutes today.

"Never regret anything that made you smile."
— Mark Twain

What is one memory/moment you always reminisce about?

DATE:_____

Before you begin, close your eyes and take three deep breaths to relax yourself.

WRITE 3 THINGS YOU ARE GRATEFUL FOR TODAY AND WHY. THEN WRITE AN AFFIRMATION TO GO WITH EACH GRATITUDE.

1. I am so grateful for _____

_____

I am _____

_____

2. I am so grateful for _____

_____

I am _____

_____

3. I am so grateful for _____

_____

I am _____

_____

READ EACH ONE 3 TIMES!

**FINISH THIS SENTENCE:
I LOVE...**

ABOUT MY DAY:

MY FAVOURITE BOOK IS:

"Today is your opportunity to build the tomorrow you want."
— *Ken Poirot*

What goals would you like to achieve by this time next year? Are you working towards those now? What can you do to achieve those goals?

DATE:_____

Before you begin, close your eyes and take three deep breaths to relax yourself.

WRITE 3 THINGS YOU ARE GRATEFUL FOR TODAY AND WHY. THEN WRITE AN AFFIRMATION TO GO WITH EACH GRATITUDE.

1. I am so grateful for _____

_____

I am _____

_____

2. I am so grateful for _____

_____

I am _____

_____

3. I am so grateful for _____

_____

I am _____

_____

READ EACH ONE 3 TIMES!

HOW DO I FEEL RIGHT NOW?

ABOUT MY DAY:

MY FAVOURITE QUOTE IS...

"I choose to make the rest of my life, the best of my life."
— Louise Hay

How have you changed over the last year? Did something or someone inspire these changes?

DATE:_____

Before you begin, close your eyes and take three deep breaths to relax yourself.

WRITE 3 THINGS YOU ARE GRATEFUL FOR TODAY AND WHY. THEN WRITE AN AFFIRMATION TO GO WITH EACH GRATITUDE.

1. I am so grateful for _____

_____

I am _____

_____

2. I am so grateful for _____

_____

I am _____

_____

3. I am so grateful for _____

_____

I am _____

_____

READ EACH ONE 3 TIMES!

TODAY I WANT TO...

ABOUT MY DAY:

ONE COMPLIMENT I WANT TO GIVE MYSELF TODAY IS:

"Yesterday I was clever, so I wanted to change the world. Today I am wise, so I am changing myself." — Rumi

Write a love letter to yourself. Thank yourself for the good you do and have done. Thank your body for carrying you and keeping you alive.

DATE:_____

Before you begin, close your eyes and take three deep breaths to relax yourself.

WRITE 3 THINGS YOU ARE GRATEFUL FOR TODAY AND WHY. THEN WRITE AN AFFIRMATION TO GO WITH EACH GRATITUDE.

1. I am so grateful for _____
_____

I am _____
_____

2. I am so grateful for _____
_____

I am _____
_____

3. I am so grateful for _____
_____

I am _____
_____

READ EACH ONE 3 TIMES!

MY AGE NOW:

ABOUT MY DAY:

MY FAVOURITE AGE TO BE:

"And, when you want something, all the universe conspires in helping."
— Paulo Coelho

Write about an event that still brings up negative emotions. Can you forgive yourself and all those who were involved?

DATE:_____

Before you begin, close your eyes and take three deep breaths to relax yourself.

WRITE 3 THINGS YOU ARE GRATEFUL FOR TODAY AND WHY. THEN WRITE AN AFFIRMATION TO GO WITH EACH GRATITUDE.

1. I am so grateful for _____
_____

I am _____
_____

2. I am so grateful for _____
_____

I am _____
_____

3. I am so grateful for _____
_____

I am _____
_____

READ EACH ONE 3 TIMES!

DID I ACHIEVE MY GOAL FOR THE WEEK?	ABOUT MY DAY:
ONE AMAZING THING THAT HAPPENED IN THE LAST 7 DAYS?	

"I have not failed. I've just found 10,000 ways that won't work."
— Thomas A. Edison

What do you want to do more of in life that you feel like you don't get time to do?

_____
_____
_____
_____
_____
_____
_____
_____
_____
_____
_____
_____
_____
_____
_____
_____
_____
_____
_____
_____
_____
_____
_____
_____
_____
_____
_____
_____

DATE:_____

Before you begin, close your eyes and take three deep breaths to relax yourself.

WRITE 3 THINGS YOU ARE GRATEFUL FOR TODAY AND WHY. THEN WRITE AN AFFIRMATION TO GO WITH EACH GRATITUDE.

1. I am so grateful for _____
_____

I am _____
_____

2. I am so grateful for _____
_____

I am _____
_____

3. I am so grateful for _____
_____

I am _____
_____

READ EACH ONE 3 TIMES!

TODAY I AM PROUD OF MYSELF FOR:

ABOUT MY DAY:

MY GOAL FOR THIS WEEK IS:

"Stop being afraid of what could go wrong, and start being excited about what could go right." — Tony Robbins

What physical features are your most favorite? What physical features are you most self-conscious about? How could you make peace with those?

DATE:_____

Before you begin, close your eyes and take three deep breaths to relax yourself.

WRITE 3 THINGS YOU ARE GRATEFUL FOR TODAY AND WHY. THEN WRITE AN AFFIRMATION TO GO WITH EACH GRATITUDE.

1. I am so grateful for _____
_____
I am _____
_____

2. I am so grateful for _____
_____
I am _____
_____

3. I am so grateful for _____
_____
I am _____
_____

READ EACH ONE 3 TIMES!

WHAT CAN/DID I DO FOR SELF-CARE TODAY?	ABOUT MY DAY:

TASK OF THE DAY:

Holding a glass of water in your hands, say your gratitude and affirmations before drinking it.

"Everything is hard before it is easy"
— Goethe

What are some accomplishments that you are really proud of yourself for?

DATE:_____

Before you begin, close your eyes and take three deep breaths to relax yourself.

WRITE 3 THINGS YOU ARE GRATEFUL FOR TODAY AND WHY. THEN WRITE AN AFFIRMATION TO GO WITH EACH GRATITUDE.

1. I am so grateful for _____
_____
I am _____
_____

2. I am so grateful for _____
_____
I am _____
_____

3. I am so grateful for _____
_____
I am _____
_____

READ EACH ONE 3 TIMES!

FINISH THIS SENTENCE:
I LOVE...

ABOUT MY DAY:

MY FAVOURITE TIME OF THE DAY IS:

"Live as if you were to die tomorrow. Learn as if you were to live forever."
— *Gandhi*

Look outside. What is the weather like right now (rainy, sunny, cloudy, windy, cold, etc) What do you like about this weather? What do you dislike about this weather? Any specific emotions you feel?

DATE:_____

Before you begin, close your eyes and take three deep breaths to relax yourself.

WRITE 3 THINGS YOU ARE GRATEFUL FOR TODAY AND WHY. THEN WRITE AN AFFIRMATION TO GO WITH EACH GRATITUDE.

1. I am so grateful for _____
_____

I am _____
_____

2. I am so grateful for _____
_____

I am _____
_____

3. I am so grateful for _____
_____

I am _____
_____

READ EACH ONE 3 TIMES!

HOW DO I FEEL RIGHT NOW?

ABOUT MY DAY:

MY FAVOURITE DAY OF THE WEEK IS:

"The journey of a thousand miles begins with one step."
— *Lao Tzu*

When you are feeling down, what do you do to cheer yourself up? Is there someone who you talk to on your down days?

DATE:_____

Before you begin, close your eyes and take three deep breaths to relax yourself.

WRITE 3 THINGS YOU ARE GRATEFUL FOR TODAY AND WHY. THEN WRITE AN AFFIRMATION TO GO WITH EACH GRATITUDE.

1. I am so grateful for _____
_____

I am _____
_____

2. I am so grateful for _____
_____

I am _____
_____

3. I am so grateful for _____
_____

I am _____
_____

READ EACH ONE 3 TIMES!

TODAY I WANT TO...	ABOUT MY DAY:

ONE COMPLIMENT I WANT TO GIVE MYSELF TODAY IS:

"Bravery is not the absence of fear. Bravery is the ability to operate effectively even while totally terrified." — Stuart Wilde

Was there a time when you mistreated someone? How do you feel about your behavior? What would you like to say to the person now?

_____
_____
_____
_____
_____
_____
_____
_____
_____
_____
_____
_____
_____
_____
_____
_____
_____
_____
_____
_____
_____
_____
_____
_____
_____
_____
_____
_____
_____
_____
_____

DATE:_____

Before you begin, close your eyes and take three deep breaths to relax yourself.

WRITE 3 THINGS YOU ARE GRATEFUL FOR TODAY AND WHY. THEN WRITE AN AFFIRMATION TO GO WITH EACH GRATITUDE.

1. I am so grateful for _____
_____
I am _____
_____

2. I am so grateful for _____
_____
I am _____
_____

3. I am so grateful for _____
_____
I am _____
_____

READ EACH ONE 3 TIMES!

ARE YOU A MORNING OR NIGHT PERSON?

ABOUT MY DAY:

INTROVERT OR EXTROVERT?

"There are secret opportunities hidden inside every failure."
— Sophia Amoruso

Write a letter to someone you miss.

DATE:_____

Before you begin, close your eyes and take three deep breaths to relax yourself.

WRITE 3 THINGS YOU ARE GRATEFUL FOR TODAY AND WHY. THEN WRITE AN AFFIRMATION TO GO WITH EACH GRATITUDE.

1. I am so grateful for _____
_____

I am _____
_____

2. I am so grateful for _____
_____

I am _____
_____

3. I am so grateful for _____
_____

I am _____
_____

READ EACH ONE 3 TIMES!

DID I ACHIEVE MY GOAL FOR THE WEEK?

ABOUT MY DAY:

ONE AMAZING THING THAT HAPPENED IN THE LAST 7 DAYS?

"You only live once, but if you do it right, once is enough."
— Mae West

21-day journey review. Write about the changes that you have made or experienced in this 21-day journaling challenge.

You have officially completed 21 entries in this journal.

I believe that each accomplishment, regardless of how small or big it is, should be celebrated.

Today it's time to celebrate you because you deserve it! Treat yourself, whether it be watching a movie, going out for a walk, or whatever it is that makes you happy...you owe it to yourself!

21-DAY journaling challenge #2

DATE:_____

Before you begin, close your eyes and take three deep breaths to relax yourself.

WRITE 3 THINGS YOU ARE GRATEFUL FOR TODAY AND WHY. THEN WRITE AN AFFIRMATION TO GO WITH EACH GRATITUDE.

1. I am so grateful for _____

_____

I am _____

_____

2. I am so grateful for _____

_____

I am _____

_____

3. I am so grateful for _____

_____

I am _____

_____

READ EACH ONE 3 TIMES!

TODAY I AM PROUD OF MYSELF FOR:

ABOUT MY DAY:

MY GOAL FOR THIS WEEK IS:

"Your biggest commitment must always be to yourself."
— Bridgett Devoue

Is there anyone from your family and friends that you would trade places with? Why?

DATE:_____

Before you begin, close your eyes and take three deep breaths to relax yourself.

WRITE 3 THINGS YOU ARE GRATEFUL FOR TODAY AND WHY. THEN WRITE AN AFFIRMATION TO GO WITH EACH GRATITUDE.

1. I am so grateful for _____
_____

I am _____
_____

2. I am so grateful for _____
_____

I am _____
_____

3. I am so grateful for _____
_____

I am _____
_____

READ EACH ONE 3 TIMES!

ONE THING THAT I WANT TO CHANGE OR IMPROVE ABOUT MYSELF BY THE END OF THE 21-DAY CHALLENGE:

ABOUT MY DAY:

TASK OF THE DAY:

Do something creative today. You can paint, draw, colour, write....whatever you consider to be art.

"Be more concerned with your character than your reputation, because your character is what you really are, while your reputation is merely what others think you are.."
— John Wooden

Describe your perfect day at the beach. Would you take anyone with you? If so, who? Activities? Food?

DATE:_____

Before you begin, close your eyes and take three deep breaths to relax yourself.

WRITE 3 THINGS YOU ARE GRATEFUL FOR TODAY AND WHY. THEN WRITE AN AFFIRMATION TO GO WITH EACH GRATITUDE.

1. I am so grateful for _____
_____

I am _____
_____

2. I am so grateful for _____
_____

I am _____
_____

3. I am so grateful for _____
_____

I am _____
_____

READ EACH ONE 3 TIMES!

FINISH THIS SENTENCE: I LOVE...

ABOUT MY DAY:

MY FAVOURITE VACATION DESTINATION:

"A person who never made a mistake never tried anything new."
- Albert Einstein

Is there a certain topic that you consider yourself to be an expert in? Or is there a topic that you would like to be an expert in?

DATE:_____

Before you begin, close your eyes and take three deep breaths to relax yourself.

WRITE 3 THINGS YOU ARE GRATEFUL FOR TODAY AND WHY. THEN WRITE AN AFFIRMATION TO GO WITH EACH GRATITUDE.

1. I am so grateful for _____
_____

I am _____
_____

2. I am so grateful for _____
_____

I am _____
_____

3. I am so grateful for _____
_____

I am _____
_____

READ EACH ONE 3 TIMES!

HOW DO I FEEL RIGHT NOW?

ABOUT MY DAY:

MY FAVOURITE MORNING ROUTINE IS:

"Kindness is the language which the deaf can hear and the blind can see."
— *Mark Twain*

What are 5 things that you want to learn about and why?

DATE:_____

Before you begin, close your eyes and take three deep breaths to relax yourself.

WRITE 3 THINGS YOU ARE GRATEFUL FOR TODAY AND WHY. THEN WRITE AN AFFIRMATION TO GO WITH EACH GRATITUDE.

1. I am so grateful for _____
_____

I am _____
_____

2. I am so grateful for _____
_____

I am _____
_____

3. I am so grateful for _____
_____

I am _____
_____

READ EACH ONE 3 TIMES!

TODAY I WANT TO...

ABOUT MY DAY:

ONE COMPLIMENT I WANT TO GIVE MYSELF TODAY IS:

"Once you replace negative thoughts with positive ones, you'll start having positive results." — Willie Nelson

What are five things that you do not like to do? What could help you enjoy doing them?

DATE:_____

Before you begin, close your eyes and take three deep breaths to relax yourself.

WRITE 3 THINGS YOU ARE GRATEFUL FOR TODAY AND WHY. THEN WRITE AN AFFIRMATION TO GO WITH EACH GRATITUDE.

1. I am so grateful for _____

_____

I am _____

_____

2. I am so grateful for _____

_____

I am _____

_____

3. I am so grateful for _____

_____

I am _____

_____

READ EACH ONE 3 TIMES!

FIRST THING I NOTICE ABOUT OTHER PEOPLE:	**ABOUT MY DAY:**

FIRST THING I HOPE OTHERS NOTICE ABOUT ME:	

"I am not a product of my circumstances. I am a product of my decisions."
— Stephen Covey

What is something(s) you wish you or someone else would invent?
Is it something that would improve your daily life?

DATE:_____

Before you begin, close your eyes and take three deep breaths to relax yourself.

WRITE 3 THINGS YOU ARE GRATEFUL FOR TODAY AND WHY. THEN WRITE AN AFFIRMATION TO GO WITH EACH GRATITUDE.

1. I am so grateful for _____
_____

I am _____
_____

2. I am so grateful for _____
_____

I am _____
_____

3. I am so grateful for _____
_____

I am _____
_____

READ EACH ONE 3 TIMES!

DID I ACHIEVE MY GOAL FOR THE WEEK?

ABOUT MY DAY:

ONE AMAZING THING THAT HAPPENED IN THE LAST 7 DAYS?

"Too many of us are not living our dreams because we are living our fears."
— *Les Brown*

Describe a time when you cheered up someone close to you. What were they going through and how did you help them?

DATE:_____

Before you begin, close your eyes and take three deep breaths to relax yourself.

WRITE 3 THINGS YOU ARE GRATEFUL FOR TODAY AND WHY. THEN WRITE AN AFFIRMATION TO GO WITH EACH GRATITUDE.

1. I am so grateful for _____
_____

I am _____
_____

2. I am so grateful for _____
_____

I am _____
_____

3. I am so grateful for _____
_____

I am _____
_____

READ EACH ONE 3 TIMES!

TODAY I AM PROUD OF MYSELF FOR:

ABOUT MY DAY:

MY GOAL FOR THIS WEEK IS:

"Failure is not the opposite of success; it's part of success."
— Arianna Huffington

How do you feel about surprises (party, gifts, visits)? Do you like or dislike them? Why or why not?

DATE:_____

Before you begin, close your eyes and take three deep breaths to relax yourself.

WRITE 3 THINGS YOU ARE GRATEFUL FOR TODAY AND WHY. THEN WRITE AN AFFIRMATION TO GO WITH EACH GRATITUDE.

1. I am so grateful for _____
_____

I am _____
_____

2. I am so grateful for _____
_____

I am _____
_____

3. I am so grateful for _____
_____

I am _____
_____

READ EACH ONE 3 TIMES!

TODAY I NEED TO LET GO OF OR FORGIVE...

ABOUT MY DAY:

TASK OF THE DAY:

Listen to a motivational podcast or TED talk.

"Change your thoughts and you change your world."
— Norman Vincent Peale

What is the most recent gift you have received from someone? What is the most recent gift you have given someone? What was the special occasion?

DATE:_____

Before you begin, close your eyes and take three deep breaths to relax yourself.

WRITE 3 THINGS YOU ARE GRATEFUL FOR TODAY AND WHY. THEN WRITE AN AFFIRMATION TO GO WITH EACH GRATITUDE.

1. I am so grateful for _____
_____

I am _____
_____

2. I am so grateful for _____
_____

I am _____
_____

3. I am so grateful for _____
_____

I am _____
_____

READ EACH ONE 3 TIMES!

FINISH THIS SENTENCE:
I LOVE...

ABOUT MY DAY:

MY FAVOURITE PLACE IS...

"I have found that if you love life, life will love you back."
— Arthur Rubinstein

What are some things you feel that you absolutely cannot live without every day?

DATE:_____

Before you begin, close your eyes and take three deep breaths to relax yourself.

WRITE 3 THINGS YOU ARE GRATEFUL FOR TODAY AND WHY. THEN WRITE AN AFFIRMATION TO GO WITH EACH GRATITUDE.

1. I am so grateful for _____
_____

I am _____
_____

2. I am so grateful for _____
_____

I am _____
_____

3. I am so grateful for _____
_____

I am _____
_____

READ EACH ONE 3 TIMES!

HOW DO I FEEL RIGHT NOW?

ABOUT MY DAY:

MY FAVOURITE COLOR IS...

"If there is no struggle, there is no progress."
— Frederick Douglass

Where do you see yourself in 5 years?

DATE:_____

Before you begin, close your eyes and take three deep breaths to relax yourself.

WRITE 3 THINGS YOU ARE GRATEFUL FOR TODAY AND WHY. THEN WRITE AN AFFIRMATION TO GO WITH EACH GRATITUDE.

1. I am so grateful for _____

_____

I am _____

_____

2. I am so grateful for _____

_____

I am _____

_____

3. I am so grateful for _____

_____

I am _____

_____

READ EACH ONE 3 TIMES!

TODAY I WANT TO...

ABOUT MY DAY:

ONE COMPLIMENT I WANT TO GIVE MYSELF TODAY IS:

"Run when you can, walk if you have to, crawl if you must; just never give up."
— *Dean Karnazes*

What is one thing that you just cannot do but know that if you did it will change your life?

_____
_____
_____
_____
_____
_____
_____
_____
_____
_____
_____
_____
_____
_____
_____
_____
_____
_____
_____
_____
_____
_____
_____
_____
_____
_____
_____
_____
_____

DATE:_____

Before you begin, close your eyes and take three deep breaths to relax yourself.

WRITE 3 THINGS YOU ARE GRATEFUL FOR TODAY AND WHY. THEN WRITE AN AFFIRMATION TO GO WITH EACH GRATITUDE.

1. I am so grateful for _____
_____

I am _____
_____

2. I am so grateful for _____
_____

I am _____
_____

3. I am so grateful for _____
_____

I am _____
_____

READ EACH ONE 3 TIMES!

3 WORDS THAT DESCRIBE ME:

ABOUT MY DAY:

3 WORDS THAT DESCRIBE MY DAY TODAY:

"If you want others to be happy, practice compassion. If you want to be happy, practice compassion." — Dalai Lama

Have you ever been on a sports team? When? Did you enjoy it? If you could have the chance, would you join a team now for that sport?

DATE:_____

Before you begin, close your eyes and take three deep breaths to relax yourself.

WRITE 3 THINGS YOU ARE GRATEFUL FOR TODAY AND WHY. THEN WRITE AN AFFIRMATION TO GO WITH EACH GRATITUDE.

1. I am so grateful for _____

_____

I am _____

_____

2. I am so grateful for _____

_____

I am _____

_____

3. I am so grateful for _____

_____

I am _____

_____

READ EACH ONE 3 TIMES!

DID I ACHIEVE MY GOAL FOR THE WEEK?	ABOUT MY DAY:
ONE AMAZING THING THAT HAPPENED IN THE LAST 7 DAYS?	

"Life isn't about finding yourself. Life is about creating yourself."
— George Bernard Shaw

What is one relationship that you would like to rebuild/improve? What do you think changed the relationship to be that way and what can you do to rebuild/improve it?

DATE:_____

Before you begin, close your eyes and take three deep breaths to relax yourself.

WRITE 3 THINGS YOU ARE GRATEFUL FOR TODAY AND WHY. THEN WRITE AN AFFIRMATION TO GO WITH EACH GRATITUDE.

1. I am so grateful for _____
_____

I am _____
_____

2. I am so grateful for _____
_____

I am _____
_____

3. I am so grateful for _____
_____

I am _____
_____

READ EACH ONE 3 TIMES!

TODAY I AM PROUD OF MYSELF FOR:	**ABOUT MY DAY:**
MY GOAL FOR THIS WEEK IS:	

"Success is not the key to happiness. Happiness is the key to success. If you love what you are doing, you will be successful." — Albert Schweitzer

If you knew you couldn't fail, what business would you start? Would you have a partner? How many employees would you have? Describe it all.

DATE:_____

Before you begin, close your eyes and take three deep breaths to relax yourself.

WRITE 3 THINGS YOU ARE GRATEFUL FOR TODAY AND WHY. THEN WRITE AN AFFIRMATION TO GO WITH EACH GRATITUDE.

1. I am so grateful for _____

_____

I am _____

_____

2. I am so grateful for _____

_____

I am _____

_____

3. I am so grateful for _____

_____

I am _____

_____

READ EACH ONE 3 TIMES!

WHAT CAN/DID I DO FOR SELF-CARE TODAY?	ABOUT MY DAY:

TASK OF THE DAY:

No complaining for the whole day. (if you're journaling at bedtime, complete this task tomorrow.)

"Strive not to be a success, but rather to be of value."
— Albert Einstein

What do you believe is your purpose in this life?
What has made you realize this?

DATE:_____

Before you begin, close your eyes and take three deep breaths to relax yourself.

WRITE 3 THINGS YOU ARE GRATEFUL FOR TODAY AND WHY. THEN WRITE AN AFFIRMATION TO GO WITH EACH GRATITUDE.

1. I am so grateful for _____
_____

I am _____
_____

2. I am so grateful for _____
_____

I am _____
_____

3. I am so grateful for _____
_____

I am _____
_____

READ EACH ONE 3 TIMES!

FINISH THIS SENTENCE: I LOVE...

ABOUT MY DAY:

MY FAVOURITE WAY TO RELAX:

"Try to be a rainbow in someone's cloud."
— Maya Angelou

What do you think your love language is: Words of Affirmation (unexpected text/card), Physical touch (hugs/kisses), Gifts, Quality time, or Acts of Service?

DATE:_____

Before you begin, close your eyes and take three deep breaths to relax yourself.

WRITE 3 THINGS YOU ARE GRATEFUL FOR TODAY AND WHY. THEN WRITE AN AFFIRMATION TO GO WITH EACH GRATITUDE.

1. I am so grateful for _____
_____

I am _____
_____

2. I am so grateful for _____
_____

I am _____
_____

3. I am so grateful for _____
_____

I am _____
_____

READ EACH ONE 3 TIMES!

HOW DO I FEEL RIGHT NOW?

ABOUT MY DAY:

MY FAVOURITE HOBBY IS:

"The soul always knows what to do to heal itself. The challenge is to silence the mind"
— *Caroline Myss*

Are you a spiritual person? In your own words define spirituality. Describe your beliefs and how they define the way you live your life?

DATE:_____

Before you begin, close your eyes and take three deep breaths to relax yourself.

WRITE 3 THINGS YOU ARE GRATEFUL FOR TODAY AND WHY. THEN WRITE AN AFFIRMATION TO GO WITH EACH GRATITUDE.

1. I am so grateful for _____

_____

I am _____

_____

2. I am so grateful for _____

_____

I am _____

_____

3. I am so grateful for _____

_____

I am _____

_____

READ EACH ONE 3 TIMES!

TODAY I WANT TO...

ABOUT MY DAY:

ONE COMPLIMENT I WANT TO GIVE MYSELF TODAY IS:

"You don't have to see the whole staircase, just take the first step."
— *Martin Luther King, Jr.*

What is an addiction of yours? Do you consider it good or bad? Would you ever try to give it up?

DATE:_____

Before you begin, close your eyes and take three deep breaths to relax yourself.

WRITE 3 THINGS YOU ARE GRATEFUL FOR TODAY AND WHY. THEN WRITE AN AFFIRMATION TO GO WITH EACH GRATITUDE.

1. I am so grateful for _____
_____

I am _____
_____

2. I am so grateful for _____
_____

I am _____
_____

3. I am so grateful for _____
_____

I am _____
_____

READ EACH ONE 3 TIMES!

FIRST THING I WOULD DO IF I BECAME INVISIBLE:

ABOUT MY DAY:

FIRST PLACE I WOULD GO IF I WERE ABLE TO FLY:

"Our prime purpose in this life is to help others. And if you can't help them, at least don't hurt them." – Dalai Lama

What are some silly things that you do that make you feel like a kid again?

DATE:_____

Before you begin, close your eyes and take three deep breaths to relax yourself.

WRITE 3 THINGS YOU ARE GRATEFUL FOR TODAY AND WHY. THEN WRITE AN AFFIRMATION TO GO WITH EACH GRATITUDE.

1. I am so grateful for _____
_____

I am _____
_____

2. I am so grateful for _____
_____

I am _____
_____

3. I am so grateful for _____
_____

I am _____
_____

READ EACH ONE 3 TIMES!

DID I ACHIEVE MY GOAL FOR THE WEEK?

ABOUT MY DAY:

ONE AMAZING THING THAT HAPPENED IN THE LAST 7 DAYS?

"How people treat you is their karma; how you react is yours."
— Wayne Dyer

Write about what is on your mind today.

You have officially completed the second 21-day journaling challenge! That is 42 entries now!

Time to celebrate this accomplishment!

21-DAY journaling challenge #3

DATE:_____

Before you begin, close your eyes and take three deep breaths to relax yourself.

WRITE 3 THINGS YOU ARE GRATEFUL FOR TODAY AND WHY. THEN WRITE AN AFFIRMATION TO GO WITH EACH GRATITUDE.

1. I am so grateful for _____
_____

I am _____
_____

2. I am so grateful for _____
_____

I am _____
_____

3. I am so grateful for _____
_____

I am _____
_____

READ EACH ONE 3 TIMES!

TODAY I AM PROUD OF MYSELF FOR:

ABOUT MY DAY:

MY GOAL FOR THIS WEEK IS:

"The most precious gift we can offer others is our presence. When our mindfulness embraces those we love, they will bloom like flowers." —Thich Nhat Hanh

What do you think is the secret to success? How do you succeed in the goals you set for yourself?

DATE:_____

Before you begin, close your eyes and take three deep breaths to relax yourself.

WRITE 3 THINGS YOU ARE GRATEFUL FOR TODAY AND WHY. THEN WRITE AN AFFIRMATION TO GO WITH EACH GRATITUDE.

1. I am so grateful for _____

I am _____

2. I am so grateful for _____

I am _____

3. I am so grateful for _____

I am _____

READ EACH ONE 3 TIMES!

ONE THING THAT I WANT TO CHANGE OR IMPROVE ABOUT MYSELF BY THE END OF THE 21-DAY CHALLENGE:

ABOUT MY DAY:

TASK OF THE DAY:

Create a playlist of your favourite songs.

"If you are not willing to learn, no one can help you. If you are determined to learn, no one can stop you." —Zig Ziglar.

What are 5 things you think are incredibly beautiful? What evokes their beauty?

DATE:_____

Before you begin, close your eyes and take three deep breaths to relax yourself.

WRITE 3 THINGS YOU ARE GRATEFUL FOR TODAY AND WHY. THEN WRITE AN AFFIRMATION TO GO WITH EACH GRATITUDE.

1. I am so grateful for _____
_____

I am _____
_____

2. I am so grateful for _____
_____

I am _____
_____

3. I am so grateful for _____
_____

I am _____
_____

READ EACH ONE 3 TIMES!

FINISH THIS SENTENCE: I LOVE...

ABOUT MY DAY:

MY FAVOURITE HOLIDAY IS:

"Find the sweetness in your own heart so that you may find the sweetness in every Heart!"
—*Rumi*

Write a letter to your 13-year-old self. What were you going through then and what can you say to help comfort the younger you?

DATE:_____

Before you begin, close your eyes and take three deep breaths to relax yourself.

WRITE 3 THINGS YOU ARE GRATEFUL FOR TODAY AND WHY. THEN WRITE AN AFFIRMATION TO GO WITH EACH GRATITUDE.

1. I am so grateful for _____
_____
I am _____
_____

2. I am so grateful for _____
_____
I am _____
_____

3. I am so grateful for _____
_____
I am _____
_____

READ EACH ONE 3 TIMES!

HOW DO I FEEL RIGHT NOW?

ABOUT MY DAY:

MY FAVOURITE WAY TO CELEBRATE MY BIRTHDAY IS:

"You are the universe, expressing itself as a human for a little while."
—Eckhart Tolle

What is the story behind your name? Who named you? What does it mean?

DATE:_____

Before you begin, close your eyes and take three deep breaths to relax yourself.

WRITE 3 THINGS YOU ARE GRATEFUL FOR TODAY AND WHY. THEN WRITE AN AFFIRMATION TO GO WITH EACH GRATITUDE.

1. I am so grateful for _____
_____

I am _____
_____

2. I am so grateful for _____
_____

I am _____
_____

3. I am so grateful for _____
_____

I am _____
_____

READ EACH ONE 3 TIMES!

TODAY I WANT TO...

ABOUT MY DAY:

ONE COMPLIMENT I WANT TO GIVE MYSELF TODAY:

"When we strive to become better than we are, everything around us becomes better, too."
—Paulo Coelho

If you won a million-dollar lotto tomorrow, what would you do?

DATE:_____

Before you begin, close your eyes and take three deep breaths to relax yourself.

WRITE 3 THINGS YOU ARE GRATEFUL FOR TODAY AND WHY. THEN WRITE AN AFFIRMATION TO GO WITH EACH GRATITUDE.

1. I am so grateful for _____
_____

I am _____
_____

2. I am so grateful for _____
_____

I am _____
_____

3. I am so grateful for _____
_____

I am _____
_____

READ EACH ONE 3 TIMES!

MY BIGGET PET PEEVE:

ABOUT MY DAY:

MY WORST HABIT:

"If you want something you never had, you have to do something you've never done."
—Thomas Jefferson

What are some things that you are REALLY good at?

DATE:_____

Before you begin, close your eyes and take three deep breaths to relax yourself.

WRITE 3 THINGS YOU ARE GRATEFUL FOR TODAY AND WHY. THEN WRITE AN AFFIRMATION TO GO WITH EACH GRATITUDE.

1. I am so grateful for _____
_____

I am _____
_____

2. I am so grateful for _____
_____

I am _____
_____

3. I am so grateful for _____
_____

I am _____
_____

READ EACH ONE 3 TIMES!

DID I ACHIEVE MY GOAL FOR THE WEEK?

ABOUT MY DAY:

ONE AMAZING THING THAT HAPPENED IN THE LAST 7 DAYS?

"Once you replace negative thoughts with positive ones, you'll start having positive results."
—Willie Nelson

If you could have a superpower, what would it be and why?

DATE:_____

Before you begin, close your eyes and take three deep breaths to relax yourself.

WRITE 3 THINGS YOU ARE GRATEFUL FOR TODAY AND WHY. THEN WRITE AN AFFIRMATION TO GO WITH EACH GRATITUDE.

1. I am so grateful for _____

_____

I am _____

_____

2. I am so grateful for _____

_____

I am _____

_____

3. I am so grateful for _____

_____

I am _____

_____

READ EACH ONE 3 TIMES!

TODAY I AM PROUD OF MYSELF FOR:	ABOUT MY DAY:

MY GOAL FOR THIS WEEK IS:

"Happiness comes from WHAT we do. Fulfillment comes from WHY we do it."
—Simon Sinek

What is the next large purchase you want to make? Describe it as if you have already made this purchase. Write in the present tense. Give details.

DATE:_____

Before you begin, close your eyes and take three deep breaths to relax yourself.

WRITE 3 THINGS YOU ARE GRATEFUL FOR TODAY AND WHY. THEN WRITE AN AFFIRMATION TO GO WITH EACH GRATITUDE.

1. I am so grateful for _____

_____

I am _____

_____

2. I am so grateful for _____

_____

I am _____

_____

3. I am so grateful for _____

_____

I am _____

_____

READ EACH ONE 3 TIMES!

TODAY I NEED TO LET GO OF OR FORGIVE...

ABOUT MY DAY:

TASK OF THE DAY:

Go to bed an hour earlier than usual.

"Everything you've ever wanted is on the other side of fear."
—George Addair

Have you ever been in love? What does being in love feel like? If you haven't, what do you think being in love feels like, or would feel like?

DATE: _____

Before you begin, close your eyes and take three deep breaths to relax yourself.

WRITE 3 THINGS YOU ARE GRATEFUL FOR TODAY AND WHY. THEN WRITE AN AFFIRMATION TO GO WITH EACH GRATITUDE.

1. I am so grateful for _____
_____

I am _____
_____

2. I am so grateful for _____
_____

I am _____
_____

3. I am so grateful for _____
_____

I am _____
_____

READ EACH ONE 3 TIMES!

FINISH THIS SENTENCE: I LOVE...

ABOUT MY DAY:

MY FAVOURITE MEAL IS:

"I am not this hair, I am not this skin, I am the soul that lives within.."
—Rumi

If social media didn't exist, how would you spend that time?

DATE:_____

Before you begin, close your eyes and take three deep breaths to relax yourself.

WRITE 3 THINGS YOU ARE GRATEFUL FOR TODAY AND WHY. THEN WRITE AN AFFIRMATION TO GO WITH EACH GRATITUDE.

1. I am so grateful for _____
_____

I am _____
_____

2. I am so grateful for _____
_____

I am _____
_____

3. I am so grateful for _____
_____

I am _____
_____

READ EACH ONE 3 TIMES!

HOW DO I FEEL RIGHT NOW?

ABOUT MY DAY:

MY FAVOURITE DESSERT IS:

"If the only tool you have is a hammer, you tend to see every problem as a nail."
—Abraham Maslow

If it were your last day in this life and you had the chance to say something just before, what would you say? What advice would you give to those around you? Any regrets you feel like you would have?

DATE: _____

Before you begin, close your eyes and take three deep breaths to relax yourself.

WRITE 3 THINGS YOU ARE GRATEFUL FOR TODAY AND WHY. THEN WRITE AN AFFIRMATION TO GO WITH EACH GRATITUDE.

1. I am so grateful for _____
   _____

   I am _____
   _____

2. I am so grateful for _____
   _____

   I am _____
   _____

3. I am so grateful for _____
   _____

   I am _____
   _____

READ EACH ONE 3 TIMES!

TODAY I WANT TO...

ABOUT MY DAY:

ONE COMPLIMENT I WANT TO GIVE MYSELF TODAY IS:

"Be miserable. Or motivate yourself. Whatever has to be done, it's always your choice."
—Wayne Dyer

How do you feel about the universe? What do you think is out there? Is it exactly as we have been taught or do you see the universe differently?

DATE:_____

Before you begin, close your eyes and take three deep breaths to relax yourself.

WRITE 3 THINGS YOU ARE GRATEFUL FOR TODAY AND WHY. THEN WRITE AN AFFIRMATION TO GO WITH EACH GRATITUDE.

1. I am so grateful for _____

_____

I am _____

_____

2. I am so grateful for _____

_____

I am _____

_____

3. I am so grateful for _____

_____

I am _____

_____

READ EACH ONE 3 TIMES!

ONE THING THAT INSTANTLY MAKES ME SMILE:	**ABOUT MY DAY:**
ONE THING THAT INSTANTLY MAKES ME UPSET:	

"The more grateful you are, the more you get to be grateful about. It's that simple."
—*Bob Proctor*

Do you believe that you create your own reality? Do you believe that everything that is happening or has happened in your life is all you? Why or why not?

DATE:_____

Before you begin, close your eyes and take three deep breaths to relax yourself.

WRITE 3 THINGS YOU ARE GRATEFUL FOR TODAY AND WHY. THEN WRITE AN AFFIRMATION TO GO WITH EACH GRATITUDE.

1. I am so grateful for _____

_____

I am _____

_____

2. I am so grateful for _____

_____

I am _____

_____

3. I am so grateful for _____

_____

I am _____

_____

READ EACH ONE 3 TIMES!

DID I ACHIEVE MY GOAL FOR THE WEEK?

ABOUT MY DAY:

ONE AMAZING THING THAT HAPPENED IN THE LAST 7 DAYS?

"Do something today that your future self will thank you for."
—Unknown

Pick one goal that you have. Now write it out as if you have accomplished this goal. Describe every detail. Write how you are feeling/acting.

DATE:_____

Before you begin, close your eyes and take three deep breaths to relax yourself.

WRITE 3 THINGS YOU ARE GRATEFUL FOR TODAY AND WHY. THEN WRITE AN AFFIRMATION TO GO WITH EACH GRATITUDE.

1. I am so grateful for _____
_____

I am _____
_____

2. I am so grateful for _____
_____

I am _____
_____

3. I am so grateful for _____
_____

I am _____
_____

READ EACH ONE 3 TIMES!

TODAY I AM PROUD OF MYSELF FOR:	ABOUT MY DAY:
MY GOAL FOR THIS WEEK IS:	

"Believe in yourself so strongly that the world can't help but believe in you too."
—Unknown

Do you do things for yourself or to please others? Explain.

DATE: _____

Before you begin, close your eyes and take three deep breaths to relax yourself.

WRITE 3 THINGS YOU ARE GRATEFUL FOR TODAY AND WHY. THEN WRITE AN AFFIRMATION TO GO WITH EACH GRATITUDE.

1. I am so grateful for _____
_____

I am _____
_____

2. I am so grateful for _____
_____

I am _____
_____

3. I am so grateful for _____
_____

I am _____
_____

READ EACH ONE 3 TIMES!

WHAT CAN/DID I DO FOR SELF-CARE TODAY?	**ABOUT MY DAY:**

Task of the Day:

Holding a glass of water in your hands, say your gratitude and affirmations before drinking it.

"Life becomes easier when you learn to accept an apology you never got."
—Robert Brault

What is the nicest/most thoughtful thing anyone has ever done for you or said to you? Why did this mean so much to you?

DATE:_____

Before you begin, close your eyes and take three deep breaths to relax yourself.

WRITE 3 THINGS YOU ARE GRATEFUL FOR TODAY AND WHY. THEN WRITE AN AFFIRMATION TO GO WITH EACH GRATITUDE.

1. I am so grateful for _____

I am _____

2. I am so grateful for _____

I am _____

3. I am so grateful for _____

I am _____

READ EACH ONE 3 TIMES!

FINISH THIS SENTENCE:
I LOVE...

ABOUT MY DAY:

MY FAVOURITE PIECE OF JEWELRY IS:

"Kindness makes you the most beautiful person in the world, no matter what you look like."
— *Unknown*

Sit quietly and just think for 5 minutes. What are the thoughts that are going through your mind?

DATE: _____

Before you begin, close your eyes and take three deep breaths to relax yourself.

WRITE 3 THINGS YOU ARE GRATEFUL FOR TODAY AND WHY. THEN WRITE AN AFFIRMATION TO GO WITH EACH GRATITUDE.

1. I am so grateful for _____

_____

I am _____

_____

2. I am so grateful for _____

_____

I am _____

_____

3. I am so grateful for _____

_____

I am _____

_____

READ EACH ONE 3 TIMES!

HOW DO I FEEL RIGHT NOW?

ABOUT MY DAY:

MY FAVOURITE OUTFIT IS:

"Be kind to all creatures; this is the true religion."
— Buddha

Describe how you would want your everyday morning routine to look like.
Why isn't your morning routine like that now?

DATE:_____

Before you begin, close your eyes and take three deep breaths to relax yourself.

WRITE 3 THINGS YOU ARE GRATEFUL FOR TODAY AND WHY. THEN WRITE AN AFFIRMATION TO GO WITH EACH GRATITUDE.

1. I am so grateful for _____

_____

I am _____

_____

2. I am so grateful for _____

_____

I am _____

_____

3. I am so grateful for _____

_____

I am _____

_____

READ EACH ONE 3 TIMES!

TODAY I WANT TO...

ABOUT MY DAY:

ONE COMPLIMENT I WANT TO GIVE MYSELF TODAY IS:

"Why compare yourself with others? No one in the entire world can do a better job of being you than you." — Unknown

List 5 things that you have done for someone that makes you feel good about yourself.

DATE:_____

Before you begin, close your eyes and take three deep breaths to relax yourself.

WRITE 3 THINGS YOU ARE GRATEFUL FOR TODAY AND WHY. THEN WRITE AN AFFIRMATION TO GO WITH EACH GRATITUDE.

1. I am so grateful for _____

_____

I am _____

_____

2. I am so grateful for _____

_____

I am _____

_____

3. I am so grateful for _____

_____

I am _____

_____

READ EACH ONE 3 TIMES!

**WHICH ONE DO I PREFER:
WINTER OR SUMMER?**

ABOUT MY DAY:

**WHICH ONE DO I PREFER:
COLD BEVERAGE OR HOT BEVERAGE?**

"Gratitude makes sense of our past, brings peace for today, and creates a vision for tomorrow." —Melody Beattie

When are you most inspired and motivated?

DATE:_____

Before you begin, close your eyes and take three deep breaths to relax yourself.

WRITE 3 THINGS YOU ARE GRATEFUL FOR TODAY AND WHY. THEN WRITE AN AFFIRMATION TO GO WITH EACH GRATITUDE.

1. I am so grateful for _____

_____

I am _____

_____

2. I am so grateful for _____

_____

I am _____

_____

3. I am so grateful for _____

_____

I am _____

_____

READ EACH ONE 3 TIMES!

DID I ACHIEVE MY GOAL FOR THE WEEK?

ONE AMAZING THING THAT HAPPENED IN THE LAST 7 DAYS?

ABOUT MY DAY:

"When life is sweet, say thank you and celebrate, when life is bitter, say thank you and grow." — Unknown

Write about what is on your mind today.

You have officially completed the 21-day journaling challenge. That's 63 entries in this journal!

Pick your way to celebrate this accomplishment because you deserve it!

21-DAY journaling challenge #4

DATE:_____

Before you begin, close your eyes and take three deep breaths to relax yourself.

WRITE 3 THINGS YOU ARE GRATEFUL FOR TODAY AND WHY. THEN WRITE AN AFFIRMATION TO GO WITH EACH GRATITUDE.

1. I am so grateful for _____
_____

I am _____
_____

2. I am so grateful for _____
_____

I am _____
_____

3. I am so grateful for _____
_____

I am _____
_____

READ EACH ONE 3 TIMES!

TODAY I AM PROUD OF MYSELF FOR:

ABOUT MY DAY:

MY GOAL FOR THIS WEEK IS:

"Nothing in life is to be feared, it is only to be understood. Now is the time to understand more, so that we may fear less." — Marie Curie

What do you think Déjà vu is? Have you ever experienced it? What was it about?

DATE:_____

Before you begin, close your eyes and take three deep breaths to relax yourself.

WRITE 3 THINGS YOU ARE GRATEFUL FOR TODAY AND WHY. THEN WRITE AN AFFIRMATION TO GO WITH EACH GRATITUDE.

1. I am so grateful for _____
_____

I am _____
_____

2. I am so grateful for _____
_____

I am _____
_____

3. I am so grateful for _____
_____

I am _____
_____

READ EACH ONE 3 TIMES!

ONE THING THAT I WANT TO CHANGE OR IMPROVE ABOUT MYSELF BY THE END OF THE 21-DAY CHALLENGE:

ABOUT MY DAY:

TASK OF THE DAY:

Go for a 20 minute walk outside. (if you're journaling at bedtime, complete this task tomorrow.)

"Life is a mirror and will reflect back to the thinker what he thinks into it."
— Ernest Holmes

If you could plan a special event, what would it be, and for who? Who would be on the guestlist? What type of decor and food would you have? Venue?

DATE:_____

Before you begin, close your eyes and take three deep breaths to relax yourself.

WRITE 3 THINGS YOU ARE GRATEFUL FOR TODAY AND WHY. THEN WRITE AN AFFIRMATION TO GO WITH EACH GRATITUDE.

1. I am so grateful for _____
_____

I am _____
_____

2. I am so grateful for _____
_____

I am _____
_____

3. I am so grateful for _____
_____

I am _____
_____

READ EACH ONE 3 TIMES!

FINISH THIS SENTENCE: I LOVE…

ABOUT MY DAY:

MY FAVOURITE SMELL/PERFUME:

"You can't go back and change the beginning, but you can start where you are and change the ending." — C. S. Lewis

List some ways that you can or already do show people in your life how much you care about them.

DATE:_____

Before you begin, close your eyes and take three deep breaths to relax yourself.

WRITE 3 THINGS YOU ARE GRATEFUL FOR TODAY AND WHY. THEN WRITE AN AFFIRMATION TO GO WITH EACH GRATITUDE.

1. I am so grateful for _____
_____

I am _____
_____

2. I am so grateful for _____
_____

I am _____
_____

3. I am so grateful for _____
_____

I am _____
_____

READ EACH ONE 3 TIMES!

HOW DO I FEEL RIGHT NOW?

ABOUT MY DAY:

MY FAVOURITE FLOWER:

"Don't be pushed around by the fears in your mind. Be led by the dreams in your heart."
— *Roy T. Bennett*

Write 3 of the funniest memories you have which still make you laugh whenever you think about them.

DATE:_____

Before you begin, close your eyes and take three deep breaths to relax yourself.

WRITE 3 THINGS YOU ARE GRATEFUL FOR TODAY AND WHY. THEN WRITE AN AFFIRMATION TO GO WITH EACH GRATITUDE.

1. I am so grateful for _____
_____

I am _____
_____

2. I am so grateful for _____
_____

I am _____
_____

3. I am so grateful for _____
_____

I am _____
_____

READ EACH ONE 3 TIMES!

TODAY I WANT TO...

ABOUT MY DAY:

ONE COMPLIMENT I WANT TO GIVE MYSELF TODAY IS:

"Cry. Forgive. Learn. Move on. Let your tears water the seeds of your future happiness."
— Steve Maraboli

What are 3 dishes/meals that you think you can make better than anyone? What is better about your dish than others?

DATE:_____

Before you begin, close your eyes and take three deep breaths to relax yourself.

WRITE 3 THINGS YOU ARE GRATEFUL FOR TODAY AND WHY. THEN WRITE AN AFFIRMATION TO GO WITH EACH GRATITUDE.

1. I am so grateful for _____
_____

I am _____
_____

2. I am so grateful for _____
_____

I am _____
_____

3. I am so grateful for _____
_____

I am _____
_____

READ EACH ONE 3 TIMES!

LAST POST I PUT UP ON SOCIAL MEDIA:

ABOUT MY DAY:

LAST POST I LIKE ON SOCIAL MEDIA:

"Only he who attempts the absurd is capable of achieving the impossible."
— Miguel de Unamuno

List 3 things that make you angry. Under each one write what you can say or do to diffuse that anger.

DATE:_____

Before you begin, close your eyes and take three deep breaths to relax yourself.

WRITE 3 THINGS YOU ARE GRATEFUL FOR TODAY AND WHY. THEN WRITE AN AFFIRMATION TO GO WITH EACH GRATITUDE.

1. I am so grateful for _____
_____

I am _____
_____

2. I am so grateful for _____
_____

I am _____
_____

3. I am so grateful for _____
_____

I am _____
_____

READ EACH ONE 3 TIMES!

DID I ACHIEVE MY GOAL FOR THE WEEK?

ABOUT MY DAY:

ONE AMAZING THING THAT HAPPENED IN THE LAST 7 DAYS?

"Don't wish it were easier. Wish you were better."
— Jim Rohn

Do you listen and follow-through when people give you advice? What is the best piece of advice you've ever received?

DATE:_____

Before you begin, close your eyes and take three deep breaths to relax yourself.

WRITE 3 THINGS YOU ARE GRATEFUL FOR TODAY AND WHY. THEN WRITE AN AFFIRMATION TO GO WITH EACH GRATITUDE.

1. I am so grateful for _____
_____

I am _____
_____

2. I am so grateful for _____
_____

I am _____
_____

3. I am so grateful for _____
_____

I am _____
_____

READ EACH ONE 3 TIMES!

TODAY I AM PROUD OF MYSELF FOR:

ABOUT MY DAY:

MY GOAL FOR THIS WEEK IS:

"My past has not defined me, destroyed me, deterred me, or defeated me; it has only strengthened me." — Steve Maraboli

Describe your dream home. Be as detailed as you possibly can.

DATE:_____

Before you begin, close your eyes and take three deep breaths to relax yourself.

WRITE 3 THINGS YOU ARE GRATEFUL FOR TODAY AND WHY. THEN WRITE AN AFFIRMATION TO GO WITH EACH GRATITUDE.

1. I am so grateful for _____
_____

I am _____
_____

2. I am so grateful for _____
_____

I am _____
_____

3. I am so grateful for _____
_____

I am _____
_____

READ EACH ONE 3 TIMES!

TODAY I NEED TO LET GO OF OR FORGIVE...

ABOUT MY DAY:

TASK OF THE DAY:

Send a thank you note to someone.

"To learn something new, you need to try new things and not be afraid to be wrong."
— Roy T. Bennett

If you were given a day to "spoil" yourself, what would you do and buy? Have you ever spoiled yourself?

DATE:_____

Before you begin, close your eyes and take three deep breaths to relax yourself.

WRITE 3 THINGS YOU ARE GRATEFUL FOR TODAY AND WHY. THEN WRITE AN AFFIRMATION TO GO WITH EACH GRATITUDE.

1. I am so grateful for _____

_____

I am _____

_____

2. I am so grateful for _____

_____

I am _____

_____

3. I am so grateful for _____

_____

I am _____

_____

READ EACH ONE 3 TIMES!

FINISH THIS SENTENCE: I LOVE...

ABOUT MY DAY:

MY FAVOURITE WAY TO COMMUNICATE IS:

"Change the world by being yourself."
— Amy Poehler

What are some productive ways you get things done? Do you make a to-do list? Set a timer for each task? What are some other ways you can improve your productivity?

DATE:_____

Before you begin, close your eyes and take three deep breaths to relax yourself.

WRITE 3 THINGS YOU ARE GRATEFUL FOR TODAY AND WHY. THEN WRITE AN AFFIRMATION TO GO WITH EACH GRATITUDE.

1. I am so grateful for _____
_____

I am _____
_____

2. I am so grateful for _____
_____

I am _____
_____

3. I am so grateful for _____
_____

I am _____
_____

READ EACH ONE 3 TIMES!

HOW DO I FEEL RIGHT NOW?

ABOUT MY DAY:

MY FAVOURITE GIFT THAT I RECEIVED IS:

"There is only one way to happiness and that is to cease worrying about things which are beyond the power of our will." — *Epictetus*

What are some thoughts and questions that come up when you think about Earth?

DATE:_____

Before you begin, close your eyes and take three deep breaths to relax yourself.

WRITE 3 THINGS YOU ARE GRATEFUL FOR TODAY AND WHY. THEN WRITE AN AFFIRMATION TO GO WITH EACH GRATITUDE.

1. I am so grateful for _____
_____

I am _____
_____

2. I am so grateful for _____
_____

I am _____
_____

3. I am so grateful for _____
_____

I am _____
_____

READ EACH ONE 3 TIMES!

TODAY I WANT TO...

ABOUT MY DAY:

ONE COMPLIMENT I WANT TO GIVE MYSELF TODAY IS:

"All our dreams can come true, if we have the courage to pursue them."
— Walt Disney.

Think about your family and friends. Who can you share comfortable silences with? Who are you not afraid to be yourself with?

DATE:_____

Before you begin, close your eyes and take three deep breaths to relax yourself.

WRITE 3 THINGS YOU ARE GRATEFUL FOR TODAY AND WHY. THEN WRITE AN AFFIRMATION TO GO WITH EACH GRATITUDE.

1. I am so grateful for _____
_____

I am _____
_____

2. I am so grateful for _____
_____

I am _____
_____

3. I am so grateful for _____
_____

I am _____
_____

READ EACH ONE 3 TIMES!

3 THINGS I CAN SEE RIGHT NOW:

ABOUT MY DAY:

3 THINGS I CAN HEAR RIGHT NOW:

"Hold the vision, trust the process."
— Unknown

What is the biggest obstacle/challenge you're facing right now? What are some ways you could overcome it?

DATE:_____

Before you begin, close your eyes and take three deep breaths to relax yourself.

WRITE 3 THINGS YOU ARE GRATEFUL FOR TODAY AND WHY. THEN WRITE AN AFFIRMATION TO GO WITH EACH GRATITUDE.

1. I am so grateful for _____
_____

I am _____
_____

2. I am so grateful for _____
_____

I am _____
_____

3. I am so grateful for _____
_____

I am _____
_____

READ EACH ONE 3 TIMES!

DID I ACHIEVE MY GOAL FOR THE WEEK?	ABOUT MY DAY:
ONE AMAZING THING THAT HAPPENED IN THE LAST 7 DAYS?	

"No one is to blame for your future situation but yourself. If you want to be successful, then become "Successful." — Jaymin Shah

If you could be a singer, what genre of music would you choose?
Write the lyrics of your song.

DATE:_____

Before you begin, close your eyes and take three deep breaths to relax yourself.

WRITE 3 THINGS YOU ARE GRATEFUL FOR TODAY AND WHY. THEN WRITE AN AFFIRMATION TO GO WITH EACH GRATITUDE.

1. I am so grateful for _____

_____

I am _____

_____

2. I am so grateful for _____

_____

I am _____

_____

3. I am so grateful for _____

_____

I am _____

_____

READ EACH ONE 3 TIMES!

TODAY I AM PROUD OF MYSELF FOR:

ABOUT MY DAY:

MY GOAL FOR THIS WEEK IS:

"You've got to get up every morning with determination if you're going to go to bed with satisfaction." — George Lorimer

Can you accept people for who they are? How do you deal with people who have different opinions and beliefs from you?

DATE:_____

Before you begin, close your eyes and take three deep breaths to relax yourself.

WRITE 3 THINGS YOU ARE GRATEFUL FOR TODAY AND WHY. THEN WRITE AN AFFIRMATION TO GO WITH EACH GRATITUDE.

1. I am so grateful for _____

_____

I am _____

_____

2. I am so grateful for _____

_____

I am _____

_____

3. I am so grateful for _____

_____

I am _____

_____

READ EACH ONE 3 TIMES!

WHAT CAN/DID I DO FOR SELF-CARE TODAY?

ABOUT MY DAY:

TASK OF THE DAY:

Act of Kindness: Do something nice for someone you love. (if you're journaling at bedtime, complete this task tomorrow.)

"Patience is not the ability to wait, but the ability to keep a good attitude while waiting." Unknown

What do you believe you deserve in life? Are you satisfied with where you are in life right now?

___

DATE:_____

Before you begin, close your eyes and take three deep breaths to relax yourself.

WRITE 3 THINGS YOU ARE GRATEFUL FOR TODAY AND WHY. THEN WRITE AN AFFIRMATION TO GO WITH EACH GRATITUDE.

1. I am so grateful for _____
_____

I am _____
_____

2. I am so grateful for _____
_____

I am _____
_____

3. I am so grateful for _____
_____

I am _____
_____

READ EACH ONE 3 TIMES!

FINISH THIS SENTENCE: I LOVE...	**ABOUT MY DAY:**
MY FAVOURITE SOURCE OF SOCIAL MEDIA:	

"Time is a created thing. To say "I don't have time" is to say "I don't want to"."
— Maya Angelou

Do you feel that you are a good communicator? Do you feel that you are a good listener?

DATE:_____

Before you begin, close your eyes and take three deep breaths to relax yourself.

WRITE 3 THINGS YOU ARE GRATEFUL FOR TODAY AND WHY. THEN WRITE AN AFFIRMATION TO GO WITH EACH GRATITUDE.

1. I am so grateful for _____
_____

I am _____
_____

2. I am so grateful for _____
_____

I am _____
_____

3. I am so grateful for _____
_____

I am _____
_____

READ EACH ONE 3 TIMES!

HOW DO I FEEL RIGHT NOW?

ABOUT MY DAY:

MY FAVOURITE WAY TO SPEND MY EVENING:

"Happiness is a state where nothing is missing."
— *Naval Ravikant*

Write about a dream you had that you still remember vividly today.
Describe it in detail.

DATE:_____

Before you begin, close your eyes and take three deep breaths to relax yourself.

WRITE 3 THINGS YOU ARE GRATEFUL FOR TODAY AND WHY. THEN WRITE AN AFFIRMATION TO GO WITH EACH GRATITUDE.

1. I am so grateful for _____

_____

I am _____

_____

2. I am so grateful for _____

_____

I am _____

_____

3. I am so grateful for _____

_____

I am _____

_____

READ EACH ONE 3 TIMES!

TODAY I WANT TO...

ABOUT MY DAY:

ONE COMPLIMENT I WANT TO GIVE MYSELF TODAY IS:

"I remind myself every morning: Nothing I say this day will teach me anything. So if I'm going to learn, I must do it by listening."
— *Larry King*

Draw a picture of something that makes you happy.

DATE:_____

Before you begin, close your eyes and take three deep breaths to relax yourself.

WRITE 3 THINGS YOU ARE GRATEFUL FOR TODAY AND WHY. THEN WRITE AN AFFIRMATION TO GO WITH EACH GRATITUDE.

1. I am so grateful for _____

_____

I am _____

_____

2. I am so grateful for _____

_____

I am _____

_____

3. I am so grateful for _____

_____

I am _____

_____

READ EACH ONE 3 TIMES!

1 THING I RECENTLY LEARNED TO DO:

ABOUT MY DAY:

1 THING I WANT TO LEARN TO DO:

"O" Your purpose in life is to find your purpose and give your whole heart and soul to it"
— Buddha

What limiting beliefs do you have that are keeping you from living your dream life?

DATE:_____

Before you begin, close your eyes and take three deep breaths to relax yourself.

WRITE 3 THINGS YOU ARE GRATEFUL FOR TODAY AND WHY. THEN WRITE AN AFFIRMATION TO GO WITH EACH GRATITUDE.

1. I am so grateful for _____
_____

I am _____
_____

2. I am so grateful for _____
_____

I am _____
_____

3. I am so grateful for _____
_____

I am _____
_____

READ EACH ONE 3 TIMES!

DID I ACHIEVE MY GOAL FOR THE WEEK?	ABOUT MY DAY:

ONE AMAZING THING THAT HAPPENED IN THE LAST 7 DAYS?

"It's not enough to have lived. We should be determined to live for something."
—Winston S. Churchill

Write about what is on your mind today.

You have officially completed 84 entries in this journal!

I hope you are really proud of yourself and celebrate this accomplishment!

Now that you have been journaling for 84 days, it's time for a journal review. List some ways that you think this journal could improve.

It's been quite a journey (84 days if you've been journaling everyday) of answering the deep-routed questions that we think about but never THINK about. I hope you know yourself better than ever before. I hope that you realize how amazing you are. I hope that you realize how powerful you are, and, above all, I hope you realize how blessed and loved you are.

You are in control of your own life. This is your journey. You are the director of your very own movie. Use the power of gratitude and the love you have for yourself to make an amazing movie, one that you will want to watch over and over again because of how good it makes you feel.

Now that you took the time to get to know yourself a little better, I really hope you love yourself more than ever before and continue to discover more about yourself.

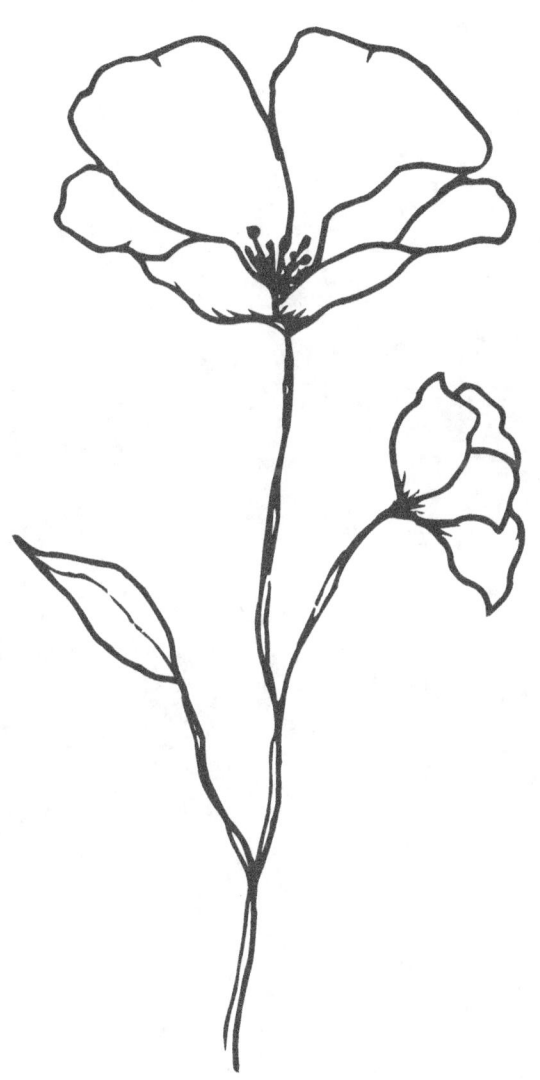